Coronary Truth

Coronary Truth

Poems by

Diane Elayne Dees

Cover design by Shay Culligan
Cover art by Nick Fewings at Unsplash.com

ISBN: 978-1-952326-42-4

Kelsay Books
502 South 1040 East, A-119
American Fork, Utah, 84003

Acknowledgments

Autumn Sky Poetry Daily: "Preparing to See the Shaman"
Poetry Breakfast: "Unanswered Question," "Lost in Space"
Amethyst Review: "Heeding Signs," "Coronary Truth," "The
    Submerged Life," "Meditation with Weights"
flashquake: "My Mother's Remains"
Better Than Starbucks: "When I Was Baptized," "Swimming
    Toward the Light"
SubtleTea: "Supplication"
Tiger's Eye: "Laura Brown Reads *To the Lighthouse*"
Postcard Poems and Prose: "The Iconography of Aging"
Snakeskin: "The Anatomy of Depression," "Winged Presence"
EcoTheo Review: "Meditation on Dusk"
Poeming Pigeon Music Anthology: "For Joni"

Contents

Preparing to See the Shaman

Should I fast and pray and drink a lot of water,
or ask for dreams? By nature, I'm a planner,
though I've never sought assistance in this manner.
Yet, late in life, I'm still the wounded daughter
who's missing parts that others take for granted;
specifically, the parts that make me feel
alive and whole, a woman who is real,
and not a she-ghost, fragmented and haunted.
I wonder if the lost parts can be found,
or if they have an interest in returning.
I pray that they rejoice upon learning
I plan to keep them healthy, safe and sound.
A shaman travels light, yet fully guided—
I hope she finds the path more smooth than I did.

Unanswered Question

There is a wall I cannot climb,
a veil I cannot pierce,
a door that will not open,
a song whose words I do not know.

How do others learn
to navigate the frigid rivers
of sorrow, age and loss?
Who taught them how to pull

the lost threads of fulfillment,
and how to gather the supplies
they need to save them when hunger
strikes, and the light dims and fades?

There is a book I cannot read,
a message I cannot decipher,
a screen I cannot see,
a secret no one will reveal.

Heeding Signs

When the snowy egret appears on your curb
at dusk, offering the cast-off fragments
of your soul a peaceful passage
through the perilous landscape of your life,
attention is required.

When the dragonfly lights on your porch,
observing your pain through multiple lenses,
granting you a chance to grasp the meaning
of that life—sit down, open your own eyes,
contemplate iridescence.

When, in your dream, the giant owl
enters your house, startling you
with its mottled feathers, remember
that something has to die so that something
can emerge. When death arrives on giant wings,
prepare to be a midwife.

My Mother's Remains

My mother seemed heavier dead than alive.
Her burned remains, barely fitting
into the sturdy funeral home cardboard box,
occupied a corner space next to the piano,
in the formal dining room near the tiny cabinet
that protects what is left of her crystal.
The light faded, the air choked us,
the neighbor's tree suddenly fell into the street,
startling passersby. She had to leave, but,
true to form, she left no wishes, no instructions,
no clues—only detritus of a deadly heat
that scorched anyone who dared to seek
the freedom to breathe pure, invigorating air.
I took most of her to a garden, to fertilize
an old found rose—one that is not at all fussy
about its surroundings. It bloomed right away,
filling me with awe, for I struggled
to grow even an inch in her presence.
A bit of her I took to London, her home,
and tossed it into the Thames. The river reached
for her, swallowing her on its way to the North Sea,
whose glacial history knows rifts even
I, born and raised in a hotspot
under continental crust, will never fathom.

My Grandparents' Ghosts

My mother's mother died when my mother
was nine; her gambler father's luck ran out,
and he died when my mother was fourteen.
My father's father's name was never
mentioned in our house. My father's mother
was a bloodless creature whose presence
told me all I needed to know about her son's
inability to connect with anything but rage.
I am a woman without grandparents.
Family stories and legends, traditions
and recipes, reside only within my DNA—
a double helix soup never stirred
by a kind woman in a warm kitchen,
never served by a gentle man
at the family table. I do not know
who they were, what they dreamed,
or how they shaped who I am,
what I dream, my brain, my flesh.
Yet I cannot live without them;
they swirl through my cells every moment,
like electric eels intent on delivering
their shocks throughout eternity.

When I Was Baptized

Sometimes, I can feel the lukewarm water
and see the abstract pattern in the multi-colored
stained glass. I was no more than eleven,
but already attracted to inexplicable patterns,
patterns that made adults uncomfortable.
I arranged the baptism on my own,
perhaps without really understanding
what it meant. My closeted Jewish mother
and atheist father were at home, performing
their rituals of fear and misery. We are filled
with water. It flows through us—our personal rivers
feeding oceans of consciousness, washing clean
the dregs of our humanity. Water heals—
fresh water, salt water, the water I drink every day.
The water of baptism doesn't mean to me
what the minister intended, yet—when I think back
to that day, and I recall the folds of white
against my tender child's skin—I am grateful.
Whatever was sacred in that water found
a tributary to my heart when I had no one
to protect me. It remains in my blood,
a filtering agent splashing against the polluted
stream of my ancestral source, creating
inexplicable channels of patterned light.

Lost in Space

The space between not wanting
to live and not wanting to die

is an amorphous island which
you alone inhabit. The coastline

shifts, the waves crash just
when you think they should

recede. The space is like a room
cluttered with Dali's melted

clocks; there will never be enough
time. There is far too much time.

The space is like Alice's rabbit hole,
and pretending to be two people

is destroying you. You cannot find
the key, so you dissolve in slow

motion while your body roams
the island, searching for you in vain.

Supplication

Baptize me in the River Ouse.
Let me sink from the weight
of my oppressive thoughts,
heavier than boulders,
breccia formed from
the landslide of my history.
My pockets forever emptied,
my skirt a dripping prism
of conflicting impressions,
I will drift into soft waves
of unknown indigo.
Lift my body, clean and light,
and let me gasp for breath
until breath
is all
that matters.

Laura Brown Reads *To the Lighthouse*

In the library, shut away from the world,
she touches books on the shelf, just as she did
when she was a lonely, frightened child.
The orpiment Canadian sun throws sparks
of colored light against the window,
and for a moment, the beauty of it holds
her still. She had not dared to read
another of this Englishwoman's books—
this woman who saw into Laura's soul, who
understood that is is possible to die.
Emptied of everything—her husband, her son
(Richie will understand some day), her baby,
her right to live in a world where lawns
are velvet carpet and women are born knowing
how to please men and bake perfect cakes—
she has already died. And so she reads
of Mrs. Ramsay, who, like the lighthouse,
is so illuminating, yet so inaccessible. Lily longs
for the knowledge that is intimacy; Laura knows
it cannot be attained. Once, on Vancouver Island,
she saw heavy fog envelop the Race Rocks
lighthouse. The foghorns blared, a warning
that light is sometimes not enough.
When the fog cleared, Laura saw the sea
eating away the ground she stood on,
and she knew that, as islands go,
she was on solid ground.

The Iconography of Aging

The razor with the rose-colored handle
and the comfort grip sits, unused, on a tray
near my bathtub, next to a bar of artfully wrapped
soap. I have reached an age when some hair
hardly grows at all, and the rest grows slowly.
I don't tell anyone because I don't want to hear
younger women say, "how great it must be
to not have to do *that* anymore." They say that
when you stop having your period, when you stop
shaving your legs, when you stop wearing
high heels. Everything is too much trouble
for them, yet I would gladly bleed, gladly click
down the hall, happily run the razor across
a streak of mango-fragranced foam.
Meanwhile, I'm not ready to move it
or put it away, this slender pink symbol
of all the inconvenience of being a woman.
It may turn out to be the last one I'll ever own;
the grieving process is slow, it cuts, and it burns.

Swimming Toward the Light

Fish in caves are born blind,
they haven't any need for sight.
Darkness is all they will ever know,
yet they easily navigate the waters.

They haven't any need for eyes,
and—having no sense of what they've missed—
they skillfully navigate the waters,
just like all the sighted swimmers.

They have no sense of what they've missed,
unlike those who once knew light,
yet—just like all the sighted swimmers—
they move toward life with every breath.

Unlike those who once knew light,
blind fish are satisfied each moment
they swim toward life. With every breath,
they thrive in fluid, tranquil pools.

Blind fish are satisfied. Each moment
for those who remember the sun—
those who once thrived in fluid, tranquil pools—
can drown the soul with cold regret.

Many who still remember the sun
now swim in frigid, hostile waters,
their souls drowned in cold regret.
They move in circles, never at peace.

They swim in frigid, hostile waters,
and darkness is all they will ever know,
while—moving in circles of quiet peace—
fish in caves are born blind.

The Anatomy of Depression

A second skin wraps so tightly
around yours that your own disappears.

It builds the self a new boundary,
while the old one dissolves like salt

trapped in polarity with water.
What was outside is now inside,

what was inside becomes a dim memory
transformed into a thick fog. You plod

through this fog, you breathe it,
believing it will kill you. But your new skin

just absorbs it, until your entire being
is left blind and gasping for the clean

air of hope, a four-letter word whose brevity
tolls in your head, while you wait for relief.

Advice I Might Have Given

A boy in a neighboring town
killed himself. "My morals,"
he posted, "are totally different
from the world around me."
If I had known him,
what could I have said to him?
"Hang on—it will get easier"?
No, because it doesn't.
You will always feel alone,
and, at times, unspeakably sad.
"Put your outrage into action"?
Yes, but do so with care—the results
are minimal, and your energy is limited.
More likely, I would have said:
Hang on, and wait for the world
around you to expand, just enough
so that, sometimes, you see
yourself in its gyroscopic mirror.
Pray, however you can, for the gift
of acceptance, and the gift of peace.
Realize that your sorrow is also a gift,
but one that you can never return.

Coronary Truth

My friend calls to tell me
he's had a heart attack.
I pace with the phone,
and through my kitchen window,
I see the season's first oriole,
darting along the lawn
as if nothing amiss has occurred.
I listen to my friend describe
the pain—the trip to the e.r., the fight
with the nurse—while a chickadee
checks out an abandoned bluebird
nest. Only this morning, I struggled
to ignore the heaving in my own chest—
the clenched fist tightened around my
broken heart that renders me breathless.
Outside, tiny hearts flutter as feathers
whir by my window, brown leaves
are thrashed, and seed falls to the ground.
My friend makes heart attack jokes,
but I know he's afraid. I am afraid: for him,
and for our hearts, no longer protected
by pure being, but rendered fragile
as hummingbird eggs by a lifetime
of confinement in human cages.

The Submerged Life

The dragonfly, unlike us, is a child
through most of life, surviving under water
for years. She learns the lessons of the wild
while molting many times. This process taught her
to recognize the right time to submerge,
the time to lift her head above the surface,
to gather wings and courage, then emerge.
Her time under the rocks is quite a preface
to a grown-up life so brief, it's here and gone.
She finds a partner and mates him while she flies,
then lays her eggs, and rises with the dawn
on iridescent wings, and soon, she dies.
The dragonfly, unlike us, is aware
that life flies on fast wings, no time to spare.

Winged Presence

The damselfly, at rest, folds up her wings
as if in prayer. She waits, perfectly still,
observing what the present moment brings.
Then silently, she holds her pose until
her instinct guides her to move on. She glides
with ease above the grass, the hills, the streams.
She has no need to stop and analyze
her path, or be concerned with hopes and dreams.
Before she is herself, the damselfly
must molt a dozen times; when she arises,
she's finished with the struggle. She can fly
unburdened by illusions and disguises.
Her jewel-like body takes up little space;
her existence is a silent hymn to grace.

Meditation on Dusk

The driven rhythm of crickets
behind sporadic croaking of frogs
mesmerizes me. Sitting on the steps
of my porch, I wonder at the glory
of all this noise. These are the sounds
of dusk, a time when, like the day,
I darken. A shiver of lost time jolts my body
like an electric shock, a ghost of a childhood
memory clutches my chest, the mystery
of nature renders me a thread of a fragment
of nothing. I am never less sure
of my existence as I am when I hear
unseen beings tear the edges of the day
from the universe, folding us all into darkness.

Master Class

Several decades in, I've gathered much advice.
Some of it was good, most of it was useless.
People see us through distorted mirrors,
and send themselves desperate warnings
in the guise of helpful suggestions. Most of what
I learned came from other sources—the cats
who taught me how to work a room, how to pose,
how to die. From the houseplants, I've learned
to quietly drop leaves when in distress, cut back
when I'm diseased, and purify surroundings simply
by existing. But my advanced degree comes
from the garden, where the same lessons are taught
over and over, for those of us who lack roots
and stems are slow to grow. The seeds teach
me patience, the bulbs and rhizomes teach me awe.
From cardinals and woodpeckers, I learn design
and construction; from squirrels, determination.
Nesting ants show me that no load is too great
to carry, while bees demonstrate the odd possibility
of forming efficient committees. The pines instruct
me that smothering is not an inevitable result
of sharing space with another; the hurricane lilies
remind me that I can still be surprised. The weeds
compel me to find a new way to look at all
the nuisances that sprout around me.
But the roses are the most demanding professors,
and we fail their lessons again and again:
Let something grow the way it needs to grow.
Not everything will survive. Nothing toxic
is ever beneficial. And the final test—
every day of your life, deadhead what is spent,
then harshly prune your desire to control what remains.

Meditation with Weights

The turf is my temple,
the sled my altar—
each white line a mala
to help me remember
my breath. I remember
my breath and my legs,
my feet and my hips,
my hands and my arms.
I remember each person
who helped heal my body.
The white lines compel me
to move on in spite of
exhaustion, sore muscles,
depression, and age.
My heart pounds a message
that life courses through me,
though I may feel distant
from life and its source.
All that I know is: keep
pushing and pushing—
reminding myself
that my breath is my life.

For Joni

The canyons echo the coyote's mournful cry
of loneliness, for which there are no words,
yet suddenly, like graceful home-bound birds,
the words appear as written in the sky.
The painted ponies dip, then leap so high,
they startle us. In silver-bridled herds,
they bear us through the grand and the absurd;
at journey's end, we still do not know why.
And yet the music calls us to go on,
amid an often misty atmosphere
that tends to blur the darkness and the light.
The melodies remain after we've gone,
as glorious reminders we were here,
though we are stardust scattered in the night.

About the Author

Diane Elayne Dees's poetry has been published in many journals and anthologies, and she is the author of the forthcoming chapbook, *I Can't Recall Exactly When I Died.* Diane, who lives in Covington, Louisiana, also publishes Women Who Serve, a blog that delivers news and commentary on women's professional tennis throughout the world. Her author blog is Diane Elayne Dees: Poet and Writer-at-Large.

www.ingramcontent.com/pod-product-compliance
Lightning Source LLC
Chambersburg PA
CBHW031156090426
42738CB00008B/1354